MINIATURE DONKEY CA

The complete beginner's gu
grooming, caring, housing,
raise miniature donkey as p

Sonia Hanks

Table of content

CHAPTER ONE

    Introduction

    Importance of proper care for miniature donkeys

    Overview of the guide

CHAPTER TWO

    Housing and Environment

    Suitable living conditions

    Shelter and space requirements

CHAPTER THREE

    Access to clean water and food

    Feeding guidelines

    Different kinds of hay, grains, and supplements

CHAPTER FOUR

    Grooming and Hygiene

    Regular grooming routine

CHAPTER FIVE

    Preventive measures

    Parasite control

CHAPTER SIX

    The significance of exercises

    Training and socialization

CHAPTER SEVEN

    Health and Medical Needs

- Common health challenges
- Symptoms of an illness
- Treatment options
- The significance of receiving veterinarian care
- Preventative steps and procedures
- Final tips and advice for miniature donkey care

CHAPTER ONE

Introduction

Donkeys in miniature are endearing and perceptive creatures that make wonderful companion animals. However, providing good care for them entails paying close attention to the specific requirements of each individual animal. In this detailed book, you will find advice and instructions that will assist you in maintaining the health and contentment of your miniature donkey. This book includes all there is to know about caring for miniature donkeys, including how to provide adequate living circumstances and food instructions, as well as grooming routines and medical requirements. This book will assist you in providing your miniature donkey with the highest level of care possible, regardless of whether you are a first-time owner or have been looking after these animals for many years.

Importance of proper care for miniature donkeys

There are several reasons why it is essential to provide adequate care for miniature donkeys. In the first place, it guarantees that they are healthy and in good condition. To maintain good health, miniature donkeys, like all other kinds of animals, need the right kind of food and water, as well as regular physical activity and veterinary care. Inadequate medical treatment may lead to a variety of health issues, and even death at an earlier age.

In addition, the pleasure of miniature donkeys is directly correlated to the care that they get. These creatures are very gregarious and intellectual, and they need contact with humans as well as mental stimulation in order to survive. The inability to get enough care may result in feelings of boredom and isolation, both of which can contribute to negative behavioural patterns and a decline in quality of life.

Last but not least, adequate care is necessary for the protection of both the miniature donkey and the human beings responsible for its care. Animals that have been mistreated or are otherwise unhealthy might be a threat to human health and safety, and they can even become a legal responsibility.

In a nutshell, the health, happiness, and safety of miniature donkeys and the humans who care for them are dependent on receiving the appropriate level of care.

Overview of the guide

This book will offer a full overview of the care that should be provided for miniature donkeys. It will cover all areas of their care, including their housing and food requirements, as well as their grooming requirements and medical requirements. The guide is broken down into six primary parts, which are as follows:

1. This part offers an overview of the significance of providing appropriate care for tiny donkeys and introduces the guide. It also introduces the donkeys themselves.

2. Housing and Environment - In this area, you will learn about the appropriate living circumstances for miniature donkeys, covering both indoor and outdoor possibilities. Miniature donkeys may be housed in a variety of settings. You will also get an understanding of the necessities, such as shelter and space, as well as the significance of having clean water and the suitable food.

3. Grooming and Hygiene - This part covers the grooming regimen for tiny donkeys, including washing and brushing, as well as cleaning feet and ears. Also included is information on maintaining good hygiene for

your miniature donkey. You will also acquire knowledge on preventative measures, such as the elimination of parasites and the scheduling of vaccinations.

4. Exercise and Enrichment - In this part, you will learn about the necessity of exercise for miniature donkeys, as well as the sorts of activities they love, such as walking and jogging, training, and socialisation. You will also learn about the types of activities you can do with your tiny donkey to enrich their lives.

5. Health and Medical Requirements - This part discusses the typical health problems that miniature donkeys have, as well as the symptoms of disease and the many treatment methods that are available. You will also get an understanding of the significance of having routine checkups and taking preventative actions.

6. This part concludes the book by reviewing the most important topics that were discussed throughout it and providing some concluding recommendations and pointers for caring for miniature donkeys. Additionally, it provides options for obtaining additional information.

CHAPTER TWO

Housing and Environment

The temperature of the area as well as the owner's personal inclination might determine whether a miniature donkey lives inside or outside. It is vital to provide children with living circumstances that are suited for them and fit their requirements, irrespective of where they currently reside. The following are some pointers about the surroundings and housing for miniature donkeys:

1. Miniature donkeys may be housed inside in a barn or stable as long as there is enough ventilation and the environment is kept clean. The environment should be devoid of potential dangers, such as anything that are either sharp or poisonous, as well as anything that the donkey may potentially eat or chew. The dimensions of the stall must be at least 10 feet by 10 feet, and its height must be a minimum of 7 feet.

2. Housing for tiny Donkeys in the Open Air

If tiny donkeys are to be housed in the open air, they need to be contained inside a fenced area. This will both prevent them from getting lost and protect them from any predators. The space should be large enough to accommodate both physical activity and recreational play, and it should provide easy access to potable water and a place to take cover. The protection from the elements may be provided by a shed with a run-in area or by a structure with three sides.

3. Shelter and Space Needs: Regardless of whether miniature donkeys live inside or outside, they must have access to shelter that shields them from elements such as wind, rain, and temperatures that are too high or too low. The donkeys should have adequate room to roam about freely and comfortably within the shelter, which should be big enough to house all of the donkeys. As a general guideline, you should provide

one hundred square feet of outdoor area for each miniature donkey.

4. Miniature donkeys need access to clean, fresh water at all times, in addition to the appropriate food for their size. They should have access to water that is clean and clear of any debris, and the water supply should be examined on a regular basis to verify that it is functioning properly. The diet of a miniature donkey should also contain hay or pasture, in addition to a well-balanced feed ration that can satisfy all of the animal's nutritional requirements. The quantity of feed that should be given to the donkey is determined by factors such as its age, weight, and degree of activity, and it should be regulated appropriately.

In a nutshell, it is critical to the health and well-being of miniature donkeys to provide them with appropriate living circumstances that are tailored to their specific requirements. They need to have access to clean water, nourishment that is suitable for them, and housing that protects them from the weather, regardless of whether they reside inside or outside. The space need to be roomy enough to for the donkeys to move about and play, and it ought to be devoid of any potential dangers that may cause them injury.

Suitable living conditions

The special demands of miniature donkeys and the environment in which they are kept will determine the living circumstances that are most suitable for them. When it comes to providing miniature donkeys with living circumstances that are appropriate, the following are some suggestions to keep in mind:

1. If miniature donkeys are housed inside, the barn or stable in which they are housed has to have enough ventilation and be kept

clean. The environment should be devoid of potential dangers, such as anything that are either sharp or poisonous, as well as anything that the donkey may potentially eat or chew. The dimensions of the stall must be at least 10 feet by 10 feet, and its height must be a minimum of 7 feet. Additionally, there should be clean, dry bedding in the stall that is changed out on a regular basis.

2. Housing for tiny Donkeys in the Open Air

If tiny donkeys are to be housed in the open air, they need a gated area that will both keep them safe from potential predators and stop them from straying off. The space should be large enough to accommodate both physical activity and recreational play, and it should provide easy access to potable water and a place to take cover. The protection from the elements may be provided by a shed with a run-in area or by a structure with three sides. In order to avoid accidents that might result in injuries, the flooring should be stable, level, and dry.

3. Shelter and Space Needs: Regardless of whether miniature donkeys live inside or outside, they must have access to shelter that shields them from elements such as wind, rain, and temperatures that are too high or too low. The donkeys should have adequate room to roam about freely and comfortably within the shelter, which should be big enough to house all of the donkeys. As a general guideline, you should provide one hundred square feet of outdoor area for each miniature donkey.

4. Considerations Regarding the Climate Although miniature donkeys may thrive in a variety of climates, their health might be jeopardised by exposure to very cold or hot temperatures. They have to have access to a warm shelter when they are in colder areas, and they have to have access to shade and

cool water when they are in hotter locations. In order to prevent the accumulation of heat and moisture, the shelter's design need to have provisions for adequate air circulation and ventilation.

5. Miniature donkeys need access to clean, fresh water at all times, in addition to the appropriate food for their size. They should have access to water that is clean and clear of any debris, and the water supply should be examined on a regular basis to verify that it is functioning properly. The diet of a miniature donkey should also contain hay or pasture, in addition to a well-balanced feed ration that can satisfy all of the animal's nutritional requirements. The quantity of feed that should be given to the donkey is determined by factors such as its age, weight, and degree of activity, and it should be regulated appropriately.

To summarise, in order to provide miniature donkeys with proper living circumstances, it is necessary to provide them access to clean water, nourishment that is good for them, and shelter that shields them from the weather. The space need to be roomy enough to for the donkeys to move about and play, and it ought to be devoid of any potential dangers that may cause them injury. To guarantee the donkeys' comfort and safety, the ground below them should be level, hard, and free of moisture, and the surrounding environment should be taken into account.

Choices between indoor and outdoor

The owner of a miniature donkey may choose whether or not to keep the animal inside or outside, based on their personal taste and the weather conditions in their area. When determining whether to keep miniature donkeys inside or outside, the following factors should be taken into consideration:

1. It is possible for miniature donkeys to live inside in a barn or stable as long as the environment is clean and has enough ventilation. The donkeys need shelter from the severe elements in colder areas, thus an indoor environment is ideal for their lifestyle. The barn or stable should be large enough to house all of the donkeys, and they should have access to bedding that is always fresh, clean, and dry. Additionally, the bedding should be changed on a regular basis. The donkeys' health can be more easily monitored when they are housed inside, and they also have greater access to their food and caretakers.

2. If miniature donkeys are to live outside, they need to be confined to a fenced-in area that not only keeps them safe from any dangers but also stops them from straying

out. Outdoor life is especially suited to regions with warmer weather, since this allows the donkeys to take advantage of the sunlight and fresh air. The space should be large enough to accommodate both physical activity and recreational play, and it should provide easy access to potable water and a place to take cover. The protection from the elements may be provided by a shed with a run-in area or by a structure with three sides. Living outside necessitates closer and more regular monitoring of one's health as well as their nutritional requirements.

3. Combination Living: Some owners want to provide their miniature donkeys with a lifestyle that combines both indoor and outdoor living environments. For instance, the donkeys may be kept inside during the night for their own safety and comfort, and then allowed out during the day to take advantage of the fresh air and get some exercise. This choice makes it possible to

enjoy the advantages of living both indoors and outside while minimising the negatives of both environments.

In conclusion, depending on the weather and the preferences of the owner, miniature donkeys may live successfully either inside or outside. The advantages of living inside include shelter from adverse weather conditions and access to fresh air and sunlight, whereas those of living outside are more obvious. Combination living may provide the advantages of both flat and house living. Whatever living arrangement is chosen, the donkeys have the same requirements: they must have access to fresh water, nourishment that is suitable for them, and shelter that shields them from the weather.

Shelter and space requirements

It is critical to the health and well-being of miniature donkeys to provide them with an appropriate shelter and sufficient area to roam. When it comes to housing and space for miniature donkeys, the following are some important considerations to keep in mind:

1. Miniature donkeys need protection from the elements, including wind, rain, and high temperatures, thus they must have access to a shelter. The protection should be big enough to fit all of the donkeys inside of it, and it ought to have sufficient ventilation so that there isn't an accumulation of heat and moisture within. A good rule of thumb is to give an outside area that is at least one hundred square feet in size for each miniature donkey. The protection from the elements may be provided by a shed with a run-in area or by a structure with three sides.

2. Miniature donkeys need appropriate room to be able to move about freely and

participate in natural behaviours such as interacting with other individuals and getting regular exercise. The quantity of room necessary is proportional to the number of donkeys as well as the size of each individual donkey. Each miniature donkey need to have an outside place that is between two hundred and four hundred square feet in size at the very least. It is important to enclose the outside area with fencing so that they are safe from any dangers and can't stray off.

3. Bedding: It is necessary to provide clean and dry bedding for miniature donkeys in order to ensure both their comfort and their health. The bedding need to be gentle and absorbent, and it ought to be changed on a regular basis to avoid the accumulation of waste products like urine and faeces. Straw, shavings, and pelleted bedding are all appropriate choices for bedding materials.

4. Maintenance: It is vital to do routine maintenance on the shelter as well as the outside area in order to guarantee the health and safety of the miniature donkeys. It is imperative that the shelter be cleaned on a consistent basis, and that any garbage or potentially harmful items be removed from the surrounding area. It is important to conduct regular inspections of the fence to verify that it is in good repair and does not pose a security risk.

In a nutshell, the provision of an appropriate shelter and sufficient space is critical to the maintenance of the health and well-being of miniature donkeys. The shelter should shield them from the weather and give proper ventilation, while the outside area should be walled in and large enough to allow for natural behaviours such as interacting with other people and getting exercise. Bedding that is clean and dry should be supplied, and it is vital to do routine maintenance on the shelter as well as the outside area in order to guarantee the health and safety of the miniature donkeys.

CHAPTER THREE

Access to clean water and food

It is crucial for the health and well-being of miniature donkeys to have access to clean water and the proper food at all times. When it comes to giving miniature donkeys with access to food and water, the following are some things to keep in mind:

1. Miniature donkeys need a constant supply of clean, fresh water at their housing location. The water should be changed on a regular basis to avoid the growth of bacteria and other potentially hazardous chemicals, and the water supply should be clean and devoid of any impurities that may contaminate it. A trough or an automated waterer may be used to supply water for the animals, and both should be checked on a regular basis to ensure that they are functioning correctly and that the water is safe to drink.

2. Miniature donkeys need a diet that is tailored to their smaller stature as well as the specific nutritional requirements of their breed. They need to have access to hay or pasture that is of a high quality, in addition to a supplement that is well-balanced in terms of its mineral and vitamin content. It is necessary to provide a quantity of food that is proportional to the donkey's size, age, and degree of activity. It is essential to supply the correct quantity of food since either overfeeding or underfeeding might result in negative effects on a person's health.

3. Feeding basis: Miniature donkeys need to be fed on a regular basis in order to keep their weight at a healthy level and to avoid digestive problems. They should be given food twice a day as a general rule, in addition to having access to hay or pasture at all times. It is essential to keep track of their weight and make necessary adjustments to their eating routine in order

to ensure that they maintain a healthy weight.

4. Rewarding miniature donkeys with treats is an option, but it's important to remember that too much of a good thing might backfire. Avoid eating sweets or treats that include a lot of starch or sugar, since these ingredients have been linked to obesity and other health issues. Carrots, apples, and several other fruits and vegetables make delicious and nutritious snacks.

In conclusion, it is necessary for the health and well-being of miniature donkeys to have access to clean water as well as food that is suitable for them. They should always have access to clean and fresh water, and the food they eat should be proportionate to their size and the requirements of their bodies in terms of nutrition. A consistent schedule for feeding should be maintained, and rewards should only be provided in moderate amounts. It is essential to keep track of their weight and make necessary adjustments to their eating routine in order to keep them at a healthy weight.

Feeding guidelines

When it comes to feeding miniature donkeys, it is important to take their dietary requirements into great mind. When it comes to providing food for miniature donkeys, here are some basic principles to keep in mind:

1. Hay or Pasture: Miniature donkeys need to have access to hay or pasture that is of high quality. It is important that the hay be kept clean and clear of mould and dust, and that it be stored in a hay rack or feeder so that it does not go to waste. The pasture should be devoid of vegetation that are toxic to animals and should have enough room for them to graze comfortably. A good rule of thumb is that miniature donkeys should have access to hay or pasture equal to between one and

two percent of their body weight on a daily basis.

2. Concentrates: Concentrates, such as grains or pellets, may be fed in addition to hay or pasture in order to supply extra nutrients. Hay and pasture are two of the most common forms of forage. On the other hand, concentrates should never be given in excessive amounts since over feeding may result in obesity as well as other health issues. It is possible to give them a supplement that has a whole spectrum of minerals and vitamins in order to make sure that they are receiving all of the essential elements.

3. Miniature donkeys must have access to an adequate supply of clean, fresh water at all times. They should have water available to them at all times, and that water should come from a source that is sanitary and free of any toxins.

4. Feeding basis: Miniature donkeys need to be fed on a regular basis in order to keep their weight at a healthy level and to avoid digestive problems. They should be given food twice a day as a general rule, in addition to having access to hay or pasture at all times. It is essential to keep track of their weight and make necessary adjustments to their eating routine in order to ensure that they maintain a healthy weight.

5. Obesity Is a prevalent Issue in Miniature Donkeys Obesity is a prevalent issue in miniature donkeys, and it may lead to a variety of other health issues. It is essential to give a well-balanced diet that satisfies their nutritional requirements and to check their weight on a consistent basis in order to reduce the risk of obesity in children. If they are overweight, the timing of their meals should be rearranged so that they consume less calories overall.

In conclusion, feeding miniature donkeys takes careful consideration of the requirements that their bodies have for certain nutrients. They should have access to hay or pasture that is of a high quality, and concentrates and supplements should be offered to them in moderation. It is essential that animals always have access to clean water, and feeding should take place according to a set schedule in order to avoid intestinal difficulties. It is important to provide a diet that is balanced and to routinely check their weight in order to prevent obesity in children.

Different kinds of hay, grains, and supplements

It is essential, while providing food for miniature donkeys, to choose the appropriate kind of hay, grains, and vitamins to suit all of their specific dietary requirements. Consider the following range of possibilities:

1. Hay: The forms of grass hay known as timothy, orchard grass, and brome are considered to be the finest types of hay for miniature donkeys. Because it is rich in both protein and calcium, lucerne hay may also be given, but only in moderate amounts. Hay should not include any dust, mould, or other potentially harmful impurities.

2. In addition to their hay diet, miniature donkeys may be fed a limited quantity of grains or pellets, but this should be done sparingly. Hay is the primary source of nutrition for miniature donkeys. A pelleted feed that is designed exclusively for tiny donkeys is an excellent choice. This kind of feed is available. Oats, barley and maize are some more alternatives, however it is important to remember that they should be used sparingly and in limited quantities.

3. Supplements: In order to guarantee that they are obtaining all of the essential

nutrients, it is advisable to give them a multivitamin and mineral supplement that is well-balanced. This may be given to them in the shape of a block or a powder, and either one can be mixed in with their meal. Probiotics and digestive enzymes are two examples of additional dietary supplements that a veterinarian may provide for their patients.

It is essential to keep in mind that the specific quantity of hay, grains, and supplements that a miniature donkey requires on a daily basis may change based on its particular requirements. If you consult with a veterinarian or an equine nutritionist, you may increase the likelihood that their food is well-balanced and tailored to their individual requirements.

CHAPTER FOUR

Grooming and Hygiene

Miniature donkeys should get the appropriate grooming and hygiene care in order to maintain their general health and well-being. The following are some tips to keep in mind about personal care and hygiene:

1. Maintenance of the coat: Miniature donkeys have a dense coat that has to be brushed on a consistent basis to eliminate dirt and loose hair. The natural oils in their coat are more evenly distributed when they are brushed, which helps to maintain their coat healthy and lustrous. To brush their coat, you may use a brush with soft bristles or a curry comb, and a shedding blade can be used to remove stray hair from the animal's body.

2. Hoof care Miniature donkeys require their hooves to be trimmed and trimmed regularly to avoid hoof issues such as infection and

overgrowth of the hoof. A skilled farrier should trim their hooves every six to eight weeks to keep them in good shape. Inspections of their hooves on a regular basis might assist identify any issues at an early stage.

3. Dental care: Miniature donkeys need to have their teeth checked at the dentist on a regular basis to ensure that their teeth are healthy and in the correct position. Dental troubles may make it difficult to eat, in addition to causing other health concerns. Regular dental care may help avoid these disorders.

4. Miniature donkeys have coats that are intended to clean themselves, so they do not need to be bathed as often as larger donkeys do. On the other hand, if they get very soiled or sweaty, you may clean them by washing them with a gentle horse shampoo and warm

water. It is essential to give their coat a good washing in order to prevent skin irritation.

5. Flies are a nuisance for miniature donkeys and may cause to health concerns such as skin irritation or infection if they are not controlled. Fly control measures such as fly masks, fly sprays, and fly traps may be helpful in warding off the nuisance of flying insects.

6. Hygiene of the environment: It is vital to ensure that their environment is clean and free of manure and other waste at all times in order to avoid the spread of illnesses and parasites. Maintaining a clean and healthy environment for them may be accomplished by routine cleaning of their stall or the surrounding pasture area.

In a nutshell, the health and well-being of miniature donkeys depends heavily on the grooming and cleanliness practises that are followed correctly. Brushing, hoof care, dental exams, and fly control should be performed on a regular basis to help avoid health concerns. It is recommended that they take baths as required, and that their habitat be maintained clean and clear of garbage at all times.

Regular grooming routine

The following is an example of a simple grooming procedure that may be performed on a regular basis for miniature donkeys:

1. The best way to remove loose hair and debris from their coat is to brush it with a curry comb or a brush with soft bristles. Brush their hair in the opposite direction that it grows, beginning at the top of their neck and working your way down to the rest of their body. Make sure that their tail is brushed as well.

2. Care for the hooves: Examine the animal's hooves for any indications of excessive development, fissures, or other

abnormalities. In the event that their hooves need being trimmed, speak with an experienced farrier. To remove any dirt or debris that may be stuck in their hooves, you may use a hoof pick.

3. Examining their teeth for any indicators of dental abnormalities, such as loose or broken teeth, uneven wear, or any signs of discomfort, is an important part of a dental checkup. If you detect any problems, you should make an appointment with a veterinarian.

4. Controlling flies Inspect the area for any indications of flies or other types of pests, and if required, take steps to manage them. Utilising fly masks, fly sprays, or fly traps are all potential methods for accomplishing this goal.

5. Bathing: Give them a bath as often as you feel it's necessary, using a gentle horse shampoo and warm water. Be careful to rinse

yourself completely so that you don't end up with skin irritation.

6. Hygiene of the environment: Clean their stall or the area around their pasture on a regular basis to provide a healthy environment for them.

It is essential to keep in mind that the length of time between grooming sessions might change based on the specific requirements of each miniature donkey. Depending on the kind of coat they have and the amount of exercise they have, some may need to be groomed more often than others. The best way to identify the grooming schedule that should be followed for your miniature donkey is to consult with a professional groomer or a veterinarian.

Bathing and brushing
Miniature donkeys should have regular baths as well as brushings as part of their maintenance routine. The following are some

pointers that may assist you in giving your miniature donkey an appropriate wash and brushing:

Bathing:

1. Brushing your miniature donkey can help remove loose hair and debris from its coat before you bathe it.

2. Warm water should be added to a bucket or hose before a gentle horse shampoo is used.

3. Apply a generous amount of water all over the coat of your tiny donkey. Take precautions to prevent water from getting into their ears, eyes, or nose.

4. When applying the shampoo, use a sponge or a soft cloth and massage the product into the animal's coat in a circular motion. Pay particular attention to parts of the animal that are known to accumulate the most filth, such as the belly or the legs.

5. Be careful to remove any traces of soap from their coat by giving it a thorough washing with water.

6. To get rid of the extra water that is on their coat, you may use a sweat scraper or a soft cloth.

7. You can either let your miniature donkey dry naturally in the air or you may use a towel to hasten the process.

Brushing:

1. To brush the coat of your miniature donkey, you may either use a curry comb or a brush with soft bristles. Brush their hair in the opposite direction that it grows, beginning at the top of their neck and working your way down to the rest of their body.

2. Be very careful when you go close to their face and ears, as well as their tail.

3. When shedding season is in full swing, it is extremely important to remove any loose hair using a shedding blade.

4. Comb or brush their mane and tail using an instrument that is developed specifically for horse hair.

5. Examine their fur for any indications of skin irritation, like as dryness or peeling, since this might indicate a problem.

If you give your miniature donkey a wash and brush its coat on a regular basis, you may help maintain its coat in good condition and clear of dirt and debris. It is essential to make use of mild grooming products that are designed specifically for horses and to pay attention to sensitive regions when brushing.

Cleaning hooves and ears

The habit of cleaning the feet and ears of your tiny donkey should be considered an essential element of their general maintenance. Here are some helpful hints on how to clean their hooves and ears in the correct manner:

Hooves:

1. To begin, take up your miniature donkey's foot and place it under their leg to provide support.

2. To clean the bottom of their hooves and remove any dirt or debris, you should use a hoof pick. Be very cautious not to harm the frog, which is the sensitive section of the hoof that is formed like a triangular triangle.

3. Make use of a brush with a firm bristle or a clean cloth to remove any leftover dirt or debris.

4. Examine the hooves for any indications of thrush, such as a putrid odour or discharge coming from the hoof. If the bacterial infection known as thrush that may arise in

the hoof is allowed to go untreated, it can result in lameness in the animal.

5. In the event that you see any symptoms of thrush, you should consult your veterinarian for advice about a treatment plan.

Ears:

1. To begin, position yourself so that you are facing your miniature donkey and raise their ear with a little touch.

2. Make use of a gentle cloth or a cotton ball to gently clean the inside of their ear to remove any dirt or debris that may be present.

3. Be careful not to hurt them, and steer clear of putting anything in their ear canal.

4. Examine their ears for any indications of infection, including redness, swelling, and discharge from the ear canal. In the event

that you see any symptoms consistent with an infection, you should consult your veterinarian for advice on treatment.

You may assist in the prevention of infections and preserve your miniature donkey's general health and wellness by giving their hooves and ears a thorough cleaning on a regular basis. When cleaning these delicate regions, it is critical to use extreme caution and gentleness, and it is essential to see a veterinarian if you observe any symptoms of infection or other problems.

CHAPTER FIVE

Preventive measures

You can assist maintain the health of your miniature donkey and avert future health concerns by taking preventative actions. The following are some guidelines for preventative medicine:

1. Checkups at the veterinarian on a regular basis: To ensure that your miniature donkey is in excellent health, it is important to see your veterinarian on a frequent basis. Vaccinations, deworming medication, and dental checkups are some examples of this.

2. Controlling parasites is important because your miniature donkey may have health issues due to the presence of parasites like worms and ticks. You should discuss a suitable deworming plan and strategies for managing external parasites with your animal's veterinary care provider.

3. Dental care: If your miniature donkey has dental issues, he or she may experience discomfort and have trouble eating. You should take them to the dentist on a regular basis and think about giving them dental vitamins or hay cubes to help wear down their teeth.

4. Vaccinations: Vaccinations are one of the best ways to prevent your miniature donkey from a wide range of infectious illnesses. Talk to your local veterinarian about an immunisation programme that is suitable for your region and the way that you care for your tiny donkey.

5. Clean living environment: Keeping the living environment clean is an important step in reducing the risk of infectious diseases and parasites spreading. Maintain a regular cleaning schedule for the stalls and paddocks, and always supply fresh food and water.

6. Exercising on a regular basis is one of the best ways to keep your miniature donkey in good condition and to avoid obesity, which may lead to a host of other health issues. Hand walking or turnout in a paddock are two examples of activities that may be used to give your horse some exercise and mobility.

You can assist maintain the health and happiness of your miniature donkey by engaging in preventative care and maintenance. In addition to regular checkups at the vet, parasite control, dental treatment, immunisations, maintaining a clean living environment, and physical activity are all essential components of preventative care.

Parasite control

Miniature donkeys are susceptible to a variety of health issues that may be caused by parasites. Some of these issues include weight loss and diarrhoea, while others include colic and anaemia. The following are some suggestions for protecting miniature donkeys against parasites:

1. Examination of the faeces Conducting faecal examinations on a regular basis might assist in the diagnosis of parasite infestations in your miniature donkey. Have a conversation with your animal hospital's vet about how often you should have faeces checked.

2. Deworming schedule: Your miniature donkey's age, weight, and living environment are all factors that should be considered when developing a proper deworming regimen for them. Your veterinarian can assist you with this. To assist in the management of parasites, it is important to adhere to the approved deworming plan.

3. Rotational deworming is a method of treating parasitic infections that includes switching between many different kinds of

anthelmintics on a predetermined timetable in order to eliminate as many different kinds of worms as possible. Have a discussion with your animal doctor about whether or not rotating courses of deworming medication is suitable for your miniature donkey.

4. Management of pastures: If pastures are managed well, there is a lower chance that they will get infested with parasites. Regular removal of manure from paddocks and pastures, as well as rotation of pastures, will enable for the paddocks and pastures to rest and heal.

5. Supplemental feeding: Feeding your miniature donkey hay and grain that has fallen on the ground might help limit the amount of parasites they are exposed to.

6. Controlling external parasites is essential, since miniature donkeys are prone to having issues with ticks and lice. To assist in the management of external parasites, the use

of an effective pesticide or tick repellent is recommended.

If you follow the advice in this article on how to manage parasites, you will be able to assist in keeping your miniature donkey healthy and prevent health issues that are associated to parasites. Collaborate with your animal hospital's veterinarian to devise a parasite management strategy that is tailored to the specific requirements of your miniature donkey.

Vaccination schedule

It is possible for the immunisation schedule for miniature donkeys to change based on their geographical region, their age, and their specific health conditions. It is critical to coordinate efforts with your animal hospital's medical staff in order to establish a vaccination regimen that is suitable for your miniature donkey. The following vaccines are some of the most frequent ones advised for miniature donkeys:

1. Tetanus: Tetanus is a bacterial illness that may be lethal to tiny donkeys. tiny donkeys are especially susceptible to tetanus. At the very least once every year, being vaccinated against tetanus is normally suggested.

2. The Eastern and Western Equine Encephalitis are both infectious illnesses that are caused by viruses that are carried by mosquitoes. Symptoms of both viruses include fever, lethargy, and neurological issues. Getting vaccinated against these illnesses should be done on a yearly basis.

3. Rabies is a viral illness that is lethal to both animals and people. The disease is spread by an infected animal's saliva and can only be caught from another affected animal. A vaccination against rabies is strongly advised to be administered on a yearly basis, at the very least.

4. Influenza is a respiratory disease that may produce symptoms such as fever, coughing, and nasal discharge. Influenza is a highly infectious illness. At least once every six months or more often in high-risk settings like showgrounds, vaccination against influenza is suggested.

5. The West Nile Virus is a viral illness that is spread by mosquitoes and may produce symptoms such as fever, tiredness, and issues with the nervous system. At the very least once every year, being vaccinated against West Nile Virus is strongly suggested.

6. Infected with strangles, a person may have fever, nasal discharge, and abscesses in the lymph nodes. Strangles is a bacterial illness. Getting vaccinated against strangles is strongly encouraged in high-risk settings such as fairgrounds and showgrounds, and

some people may need additional vaccinations.

Have a conversation with your trusted veterinary professional about the immunisations that are required for your tiny donkey and how often they should be administered. Protecting the health of your tiny donkey and helping to stop the spread of illness may both be aided by ensuring that their vaccines are up to date.

CHAPTER SIX

The significance of exercises

Exercising miniature donkeys regularly is essential to their overall well-being since it helps to preserve both their physical and mental health. Exercising miniature donkeys is useful for a number of reasons, including the following:

1. Weight control: Regular exercise may help avoid obesity in miniature donkeys, which can lead to a variety of health issues such as laminitis, insulin resistance, and joint difficulties. Obesity in miniature donkeys can be prevented by weight management and regular exercise.

2. Tone and strength of the muscles: Miniature donkeys may benefit from regular exercise to help them maintain their tone and strength of their muscles, which is essential for their general physical health and mobility.

3. Health of the cardiovascular system
Exercising miniature donkeys may assist enhance their cardiovascular health by speeding up their heart rates and boosting the amount of blood that flows through their bodies.

4. Mental stimulation: Miniature donkeys may benefit from the mental stimulation that exercise can bring, which can aid in warding off boredom and the associated behavioural issues.

5. Exercise may also give opportunity for miniature donkeys to socialise with other animals, which is essential for their emotional and mental well-being and is an important aspect of their overall well-being.

It is essential to provide your miniature donkey the kind of exercise that is suitable for their age, the state of their health, and the level of their physical ability. Make sure to offer safe and secure settings for your tiny donkey to exercise in, and consult with your veterinarian to come up with a suitable activity schedule for your miniature donkey. Exercise on a consistent basis is one of the best things you can do for the long-term health and happiness of your miniature donkey.

Different kinds of activities

The following is a list of several kinds of activities that are appropriate for miniature donkeys:

1. Walking: Miniature donkeys benefit greatly from engaging in regular walking, which is an excellent form of exercise for them. You may go for a stroll with your miniature donkey, either on a path or around your property, by using a lead line or a harness and taking it for a walk.

2. Free turnout is a terrific method to give physical activity and mental stimulation for

your tiny donkey. If you have access to a safe paddock or pasture, your miniature donkey should be allowed to graze freely there. Assure that the location is risk-free and devoid of potential dangers, and make sure that visitors have access to potable water and shady areas.

3. Obstacle course Constructing an obstacle course for miniature donkeys may give both mental and physical stimulation to the animals. You may train your tiny donkey to navigate over obstacles that you set up using cones, poles, or any number of other objects.

4. Light riding: If your miniature donkey has been properly taught for riding, you may give it with the necessary activity by having it participate in some light riding. Be sure to choose a saddle that is the right size for your tiny donkey, and avoid loading him up with too much weight.

5. Toys and treats: Providing miniature donkeys with toys and goodies may also serve as a kind of mental stimulation for the animals. You may give them balls, bouncy balls, or other types of toys to play with, and as a reward for good behaviour, you could give them carrots or apples.

Always make sure you have someone to keep an eye on your miniature donkey while they are exercising, and modify their level of activity according to their physical capabilities and the condition of their health. Exercise on a consistent basis is one of the best things you can do for the long-term health and happiness of your miniature donkey.

Walking and running

Walking and jogging are both appropriate kinds of exercise for miniature donkeys; however, it is essential to modify the intensity of the activity in accordance with your tiny donkey's physical capabilities and current state of health.

Walking is a kind of exercise that is suitable for everyday use since it has a minimal effect. You may go for a stroll with your miniature donkey, either on a path or around your property, by using a lead line or a harness and taking it for a walk. The physical activity of walking not only helps to preserve cardiovascular and muscular health, but it also gives cerebral stimulation.

Running is another kind of exercise that may be beneficial for miniature donkeys; nevertheless, it is essential to do this activity in a secure and regulated manner. Running should only be done in short bursts, and it is crucial not to overdo it since it might put pressure on the joints and muscles of the runner. Running should only be done in short bursts. If you want to get your miniature donkey to run faster, you may play with them or set up obstacles, but be sure to keep an eye on their behaviour and stop the activity if they seem to be getting tired or are experiencing any pain.

Always get the advice of your trusted veterinarian before beginning an exercise routine for your tiny donkey, and be sure to adapt the intensity of the workout according to your donkey's current physical capabilities and overall health. Exercise on a consistent basis is one of the best things you can do for the long-term health and happiness of your miniature donkey.

Training and socialization

Training and socialisation are essential components of caring for a tiny donkey since they assist your donkey become well-mannered and at ease in the company of people and other animals. In order to properly teach and socialise your miniature donkey, consider the following advice:

1. Get an early start: It is preferable to start training and socialisation while your miniature donkey is young, as they are more sensitive to new experiences and less prone to acquire undesirable habits in their later years.

2. Make use of positive reinforcement: Positive reinforcement is an efficient approach of training for tiny donkeys since it rewards excellent behaviour and encourages the donkeys to continue to demonstrate that behaviour. As a reward for excellent behaviour, you may give your miniature donkey some goodies or just praise it.

3. Regular handling of your tiny donkey helps it get used to being around people and to being stroked. tiny donkeys might be difficult to socialise since they are so little. This may make it simpler to provide veterinary treatment and groom the animal.

4. Introducing your tiny donkey to other animals, such as horses or goats, may help them develop strong social skills and lower the chance of violence. Socialising your small donkey with other animals, such as horses or goats, can benefit your miniature donkey.

5. Teach your miniature donkey the fundamental instructions: Teaching your miniature donkey the fundamental orders, such as "halt" or "back up," may help you maintain control of their behaviour and keep them safe.

It is important to keep in mind that you need to teach and socialise your tiny donkey with patience and consistency, and that your first priority should always be the safety of both you and your donkey. Your miniature donkey has the potential to develop into a well-mannered and kind companion with the right kind of training and socialisation.

CHAPTER SEVEN

Health and Medical Needs

It is essential for the miniature donkey's general well-being that their health requirementss and need for medical care be met. The following are some essential components of the health and medical treatment of miniature donkeys:

1. Checkups with the veterinarian on a regular basis It is essential to have your miniature donkey examined by a veterinarian on a yearly basis, if not more often, to ensure that they are healthy and to identify any possible health issues at an earlier stage.

2. Dental care: In order to maintain excellent oral health, miniature donkeys need to have their teeth checked and cleaned on a regular basis. This involves having regular dental checkups, tooth floating, and cleaning your teeth on a regular basis.

3. foot care: Providing routine foot care for your miniature donkey is crucial to ensuring its comfort and good health. This involves doing regular trimming, looking for symptoms of lameness or infection, and responding swiftly to any difficulties that may arise.

4. Controlling parasites requires regular deworming, since an accumulation of internal parasites, which may lead to major health issues, can be avoided by this practise. Your miniature donkey should follow a deworming regimen that has been established in conjunction with your veterinary professional.

5. Vaccinations: It is essential to vaccinate your miniature donkey in order to prevent them from infectious illnesses such as tetanus, West Nile virus, and rabies. Make an appointment with your animal hospital's

doctor to discuss the best vaccination regimen for you.

6. Care in an Emergency Be ready for any unexpected events that may arise by having a plan in place and being aware of how to identify symptoms of disease or injury in your miniature donkey. Always have a first aid kit and the contact information for your veterinarian on hand in case of an emergency.

You may assist your miniature donkey have a long and happy life for many years to come by adhering to the aforementioned principles and developing a productive working relationship with your animal hospital's staff of medical professionals.

Common health challenges

The health problems that may affect miniature donkeys are as varied as those that can affect any other animal. The following are some typical health concerns that should be taken into consideration:

1. Lameness is a condition that may be brought on by a number of different things, including improper hoof care, overwork, or injury. Signs of lameness may include walking with a limp, being reluctant to move, or displaying an altered gait.

2. Dental issues Miniature donkeys may have dental issues include overgrown teeth, periodontal disease, or tooth abscesses. Other dental issues include periodontal disease. Drooling, trouble chewing, or changes in eating routines might all be indications that dental issues are present.

3. Internal parasites in miniature donkeys, such as worms, may be the root cause of a range of health issues, including diarrhoea, anaemia, and weight loss. Worms are one example of an internal parasite.

4. Skin conditions: Dermatitis, fungal infections, and lice infestations are just some of the skin conditions that may affect miniature donkeys. Itching, scabbing, or loss of hair are some of the symptoms that may indicate an issue with the skin.

5. Poor air quality or allergen exposure may be the root cause of respiratory issues, such as pneumonia or heaves (chronic obstructive pulmonary disease, often known as COPD).

6. Eye conditions Miniature donkeys are susceptible to developing a variety of eye conditions, including cataracts, infections, and traumas. Eye disorders may manifest itself in a variety of ways, including cloudiness, discharge, or squinting.

It is essential to have a solid working relationship with your veterinary practitioner in order to keep close track of your miniature donkey's health and identify any possible health concerns at an early stage. Many common health problems may be avoided by maintaining a healthy diet, getting the recommended amount of exercise, and practising excellent cleanliness on a consistent basis.

Symptoms of an illness

It is essential for you, as a responsible owner of a miniature donkey, to be able to recognise indications of disease in your animal so that you may get it to a veterinarian as soon as possible for treatment. The following is a list of symptoms that are often seen in miniature donkeys:

1. a lack of appetite or an unexpected loss of weight

2. a state of listlessness or melancholy

3. Adaptations in either manner of behaving or attitude

4. rapid breathing or trouble breathing are symptoms of this condition.

5. Symptoms include hacking, sneezing, and discharge from the nose

6. Symptoms such as diarrhoea or other shifts in bowel routines

7. Indications of lameness or an unwillingness to move

8. abnormally large or many lumps

9. Alterations in urine patterns or symptoms of pain while peeing are red flags.

10. Discharge that is not typical coming from the eyes, nose, or ears

11. Symptoms such as a fever or discomfort.

It is imperative that you get in touch with your miniature donkey's veterinarian as soon as possible if you see any of these symptoms in your animal. Intervention at an early stage may help reduce the risk of more significant health issues and increase the likelihood of making a complete recovery.

Treatment options

The precise illness or injury, as well as the severity of the problem, will determine which treatment choices are available for a miniature donkey that is sick or wounded. The following are some general treatment options that your veterinarian may recommend:

1. Medication: In order to assist control symptoms and encourage recovery, your veterinarian may recommend medicines like as antibiotics, anti-inflammatory meds, or pain relievers. This will depend on the specific health condition that your pet is experiencing.

2. Surgery is a procedure that may be required to address a patient's injury or health condition in certain circumstances.

3. treatment with fluids: If your miniature donkey is suffering from dehydration or a sickness that is causing fluid loss, your veterinarian may prescribe treatment with fluids in order to restore hydration and maintain general health.

4. Care for wounds In the event that your miniature donkey gets a wound, it is essential to keep the affected area clean and to use proper wound care treatments as directed by your veterinarian.

5. Physical treatment: In some circumstances, your miniature donkey may benefit from participating in physical therapy or rehabilitation activities in order to speed up their recovery from an accident or sickness.

It is essential to have a solid working relationship with your veterinarian in order to design a treatment plan that is suitable for the individual requirements of your tiny donkey. Many health problems, as well as the need for treatment, may be avoided or at least reduced by maintaining a healthy diet, going to the veterinarian for checkups on a regular basis, and maintaining a living environment that is clean and secure.

Regular check-ups

Maintaining the health of your tiny donkey requires that you take it in for checkups on a regular basis. The following are some of the reasons why:

1. Early identification of health problems: Your veterinarian may do a comprehensive physical exam during a normal checkup in order to search for any indications of disease or injury. This can help with early diagnosis of health problems. If health problems are caught in their early stages, there is a better probability of a good treatment result.

2. immunisations: Annual examinations provide the perfect time to ensure that your miniature donkey is up to date on all of the immunisations necessary to guard against the most prevalent illnesses.

3. management of parasites: Routine faecal inspections may be performed by your veterinarian, and they can also propose parasite management treatments that can help you avoid infestations.

4. Dental treatment: If required, your veterinarian may also do regular dental examinations and provide recommendations for dental care procedures such as floating, which involves filing down sharp teeth.

5. Nutritional counselling: Your family veterinarian is the best person to provide nutritional guidance and provide recommendations for supplements, if any are required, to make sure that your miniature

donkey is receiving all of the nutrients it needs to be in the best possible condition.

6. Training and behaviour: Your veterinarian is also a good resource for guidance on training and behaviour, and may suggest other resources if necessary.

Visits to the veterinarian on a regular basis are one of the best ways to guarantee that your tiny donkey will have a long and healthy life. Your miniature donkey's particular requirements and medical history will inform the recommendations that your veterinarian makes on how often you should take them in.

The significance of receiving veterinarian care

Your tiny donkey really needs to get veterinary treatment in order to maintain its general health and well-being. The following are some of the reasons why:

1. Early diagnosis and prevention of health problems Receiving routine veterinary care may assist in the diagnosis of health problems before they progress to a more critical stage, which paves the way for earlier intervention and treatment. Your miniature donkey's health may also be maintained with the aid of preventive treatments, including as immunisations and parasite management, which can be recommended by your veterinarian.

2. Advice from a qualified medical professional Your family veterinarian is the best person to consult with on your miniature donkey's diet, its exercise routine, its behaviour, and any other element of proper pet care.

3. Access to diagnostic tools and treatments: In the event that your miniature donkey does become unwell or wounded, your veterinarian has access to diagnostic tools

and treatments that you, as the owner, may not have otherwise been able to get.

4. Support and guidance during trying times
In the event that your miniature donkey develops a life-threatening illness or has to be put to sleep, your veterinarian will be able to provide you with support and direction through these trying times.

5. Compliance with regulations: the law in certain locations mandates that some animals, such as miniature donkeys, need routine veterinarian treatment.

In general, providing veterinarian treatment for your miniature donkey is quite necessary if you want to protect their health and enjoyment. Your miniature donkey's chances of living a long and healthy life may be improved by receiving regular checkups and preventive care, as well as receiving timely treatment for any health concerns that may arise.

Preventative steps and procedures

It is essential to take preventative actions in order to guarantee the continued health and happiness of your tiny donkey. The following are some important aspects to concentrate on:

1. Nutrition: It is crucial to provide your miniature donkey with a food that is both well-balanced and fits their nutritional demands in order to avoid health concerns such as obesity, dental difficulties, and digestive disorders. Talk to your trusted veterinarian about the best food and feeding regimen for your tiny donkey so that you may get their recommendation.

2. Elimination of parasites is important for the health of your miniature donkey since some parasites, like worms, may cause severe health issues. Infestations may be avoided by doing regular faecal examinations and receiving deworming medications.

3. Vaccinations: Vaccinations are very necessary in order to protect your miniature donkey from common illnesses that, in severe cases, may be fatal. To decide the suitable immunisation regimen for your miniature donkey, it is best to discuss the matter with your trusted veterinarian.

4. Dental care: Because miniature donkeys have specific dental requirements, they may need to have their teeth floated on a regular basis (which involves filing down their pointy teeth) to avoid dental complications.

5. Exercising: Keeping your miniature donkey active on a consistent basis is essential for preserving both its physical and emotional health. The prevention of obesity, joint difficulties, and behavioural challenges may be aided by providing chances for physical activity.

6. Environmental considerations: You should make sure that your miniature donkey has

access to clean water, that it lives in an area that is appropriate for it, and that it is shielded from harsh weather conditions.

You may help prevent health problems from occurring and ensuring that your tiny donkey continues to enjoy good health and happiness if you pay attention to the important areas listed above. In addition, routine veterinarian treatment and monitoring may assist in the detection and prevention of any health problems before they become severe.

Final tips and advice for miniature donkey care

The following is some sage counsel and parting words of wisdom on the care of your tiny donkey:

1. You should educate yourself on the special requirements and behaviours of tiny donkeys to ensure that you are giving the best possible care for them. Educating yourself on

the individual needs and behaviours of miniature donkeys will guarantee that you are providing the best possible care.

2. Find a reputable and experienced doctor Look for a veterinarian who has previous experience working with tiny donkeys and who is able to give preventive treatment and regular checkups for your donkey.

3. Don't forget to give your miniature donkey lots of room to go about and plenty of opportunities to mingle with other animals and donkeys of their own kind. Miniature donkeys are sociable creatures and need enough of room to do so.

4. Check the health of your tiny donkey on a frequent basis: It is important to monitor the behaviour and general health of your miniature donkey on a regular basis in order to identify any potential health problems as soon as possible.

5. Be patient and be consistent with the training: It will take time and patience to teach your miniature donkey properly. When you want the greatest outcomes, you need to be consistent and use positive reinforcement.

6. Take pleasure in the one-of-a-kind characteristics and allure of your tiny donkey: tiny donkeys are noted for having dispositions that are both charming and lively. Spend some time appreciating and revelling in the one-of-a-kind qualities they possess.

You can help your miniature donkey have a long, healthy, and happy life by paying attention to the advice provided here and giving it with the appropriate level of care.

Printed in Great Britain
by Amazon